bridges to contemplative living
with thomas merton

eight:
seeing that paradise begins now

edited by jonathan montaldo & robert g. toth
of the merton institute for contemplative living

ave maria press AmP **notre dame, indiana**

Ave Maria Press gratefully acknowledges the permission of the following publishers for use of excerpts from these books:

At a Journal Workshop by Ira Progoff © 1975 by G.P. Putnam's Sons. Reprinted by permission.

The Collected Poems of Thomas Merton by Thomas Merton, copyright © 1963 by the Abbey of Gethsemani. Reprinted by permission of New Directions Publishing Corp.

Contemplation in a World of Action by Thomas Merton, copyright © 1973 by the Abbey of Gethsemani. Used by permission of Doubleday, a division of Random House, Inc.

The Divine Milieu by Teilhard de Chardin, copyright © 1965 by Harper and Row, Publishers. Reprinted by permission of Harper and Row, Publishers.

Entering the Silence: The Journals of Thomas Merton, Volume Two 1941–1952 by Thomas Merton and edited by Jonathan Montaldo, copyright © 1995 by The Merton Legacy Trust. Reprinted by permission of HarperCollins Publishers

Faith and Violence: Christian Teaching and Christian Practice by Thomas Merton, copyright © 1968. Reprinted with permission of University of Notre Dame Press.

"From Pilgrimage to Crusade," from *Mystics and Zen Masters* by Thomas Merton, copyright © 1967 by the Abbey of Gethsemani. Copyright renewed 1995 by Robert Giroux, James Laughlin, and Tommy O'Callaghan as trustees of the Merton Legacy Trust. Reprinted by permission of Farrar, Straus and Giroux, LLC.

The Psalms: An Inclusive Language Version Based on the Grail Translation from the Hebrew. Published through exclusive license agreement by G.I.A. Publications, Inc. Copyright © 1963, 1986 by The Grail (England). Used by permission of G.I.A.

The Roots of Christian Mysticism by Olivier Clément, copyright © 1993 by New City Press. Used by permission of New City Press.

Seasons of Celebration by Thomas Merton, copyright © 1950 by the Abbey of Gethsemani. Reprinted by permission of Farrar, Straus and Giroux.

Toward Final Integration in the Adult Personality, by A. Reza Arasteh, copyright © 1965 by Leiden: E.J. Brill. Used with permission of Schenkman Books, Inc.

Founded in 1865, Ave Maria Press is a ministry of the Indiana Province of Holy Cross.

www.avemariapress.com

ISBN-10 1-59471-241-7   ISBN-13 978-1-59471-241-8

Cover and text design by Andy Wagoner.

Cover photograph © Robert Hill Photography.

Interior photograph; Polonnaruwa, Sri Lanka (Reclining Buddha and Standing Ananda), by Thomas Merton. Used with permission of the Merton Legacy Trust and the Thomas Merton Center at Bellarmine University. Interior photograph of Thomas Merton on p. 7 by John Lyons. Used with permission of the Merton Legacy Trust.

Printed and bound in the United States of America.

I stand among you as one who offers a small message of hope that first, there are always people who dare to seek on the margin of society, who are not dependent on social acceptance, not dependent on social routine, and prefer a kind of free-floating existence under a state of risk. And among these people, if they are faithful to their own calling, to their own vocation, and to their own message from God, communication on the deepest level is possible. And the deepest level of communication is not communication, but communion. It is wordless. It is beyond words, and it is beyond speech, and it is beyond concept. Not that we discover a new unity. We discover an older unity. We are already one. But we imagine that we are not. And what we have to recover is our original unity. What we have to be is what we are.

THOMAS MERTON
The Asian Journal of Thomas Merton

A NOTE ABOUT INCLUSIVE LANGUAGE
Thomas Merton wrote at a time before inclusive language was common practice. In light of his inclusive position on so many issues and his references to our essential unity, we hope these texts will be read from an inclusive point of view.

CONTENTS

INTRODUCTION

WHAT DO WE MEAN BY CONTEMPLATIVE LIVING?

Life is a spiritual journey. Contemplative living is a way of responding to our everyday experiences by consciously attending to our relationships. It deepens our awareness of our connectedness and communion with others, becomes a positive force of change in our lives, and provides meaningful direction to our journey. Ultimately, contemplative living leads us to a sense of well-being, profound gratitude, and a clearer understanding of our purpose in life.

Living contemplatively begins with ourselves but leads us in the end to embrace deeply not only our truest self, but God, neighbor, and all of creation. By reflecting on our everyday experiences, we seek the depths of our inner truth. By exploring our beliefs, illusions, attitudes, and assumptions, we find our true self and discover how we relate to the larger community. Contemplative living directs our minds and hearts to the truly important issues of human existence, making us less likely to be captivated by the superficial distractions that so easily occupy our time.

WHO WAS THOMAS MERTON?

For over sixty years, the thought and writings of Thomas Merton have guided spiritual seekers across the world. His writings offer important insights into four essential relationships—with self, with God, with other people, and with all of creation. While the

Christian tradition is the foundation of his perspective, he is open and inclusive in his examination of other religious traditions, recognizing the important contribution of all faith traditions to the history of civilization. He drew from their strengths to enhance the spiritual growth of individuals and communities.

Thomas Merton was born in Prades, France, in 1915. His mother was from the United States and his father from New Zealand. Educated in France, England, and the United States, he received a master's degree in English from Columbia University. In 1938 he was baptized into the Catholic Church. He taught at St. Bonaventure University for a year and then in 1941 entered the Cistercian Order as a monk of the Abbey of Gethsemani in Kentucky. Directed by his Abbot, Dom Frederic Dunne, Merton wrote his autobiography, *The Seven Storey Mountain*, which was published in 1948.

For fifteen years he served as Master of Scholastics and Novices while writing many books and articles on the spiritual life, interreligious understanding, peace, and social justice issues. In December of 1968, he journeyed to Asia to attend a conference of contemplatives near Bangkok, Thailand. While there he was accidentally electrocuted and died at the age of fifty-three.

Interest in Merton has grown steadily since his death. *The Seven Storey Mountain*, which appears on lists of the one hundred most important books of the last century, has been in print ever since its first edition and has sold millions of copies. The volume of printed work by and about him attests to Merton's popularity. His works have been translated into thirty-five languages and new foreign language editions continue to be printed. The International Thomas Merton Society currently has thirty chapters in the United States and fourteen in other countries.

Thomas Merton is distinguished among contemporary spiritual writers by the depth and substance of his thinking. Merton was a scholar who distilled the best thinking of the best theologians, philosophers, and poets throughout the centuries, from both the West and the East, and presented their ideas in the context of the Christian worldview. His remarkable and enduring popularity indicates that his work continues to speak to the minds and hearts of people searching for answers to life's important questions. For many he is a spiritual guide, and for others he offers a place to retreat to in difficult times. His writings take people into deep places within themselves and offer insight into the paradoxes of life. Merton struggled to be contemplative in a world of action, yet he offered no quick fix or "Ten Easy Steps" to a successful spiritual life.

Using Bridges to Contemplative Living with Thomas Merton

Bridges is intended for anyone seeking to live more contemplatively. For some it initiates a spiritual journey, for others it leads to re-examination or recovery of a neglected spiritual life, and for still others it deepens an already vibrant spirituality. Through reflection and dialogue on specific spiritual themes, participants revisit and refresh their perspectives on and understanding of life. They explore the strength and balance of the relationships that ultimately determine who they are: relationships with self, God, others, and nature. Through examining these relationships, participants probe their understanding of life's great questions:

"Who am I?"
"Who is God?"
"Why am I here?"
"What am I to do with my life?"

The selected readings move participants in and out of four dimensions of contemplative living—*Awakening* to an ever-deepening awareness of "true-self"; *Contemplation* of a life experienced from a God-centered perspective; *Compassion* in relationships with others; and *Unity* realized in our undeniable and essential interconnectedness with all of creation. This fourfold process of spiritual formation frames much of Merton's thought and writing.

This is not a spiritual formation program in some "otherworldly" sense. Merton insisted that our spiritual life is our everyday lived experience. There is no separation between them. Bridges does not require an academic background in theology, religion, or spirituality, nor does it require the use of any particular spiritual practices or prayers. There are no levels of perfection, goals to attain, or measurements of progress. This is not an academic or scholarly undertaking. Everyone will find a particular way of contemplative living within his or her own circumstances, religious tradition, and spiritual practices.

The Bridges to Contemplative Living with Thomas Merton series is especially designed for small group dialogue. The selected themes of each session are intended to progressively inform and deepen the relationships that form our everyday lives. Each session begins with scripture and ends in prayer. In between there are time and mental space for spiritual reading, reflection, and contemplative dialogue.

WHAT DO WE MEAN BY CONTEMPLATIVE DIALOGUE?

Contemplative dialogue is meant to be non-threatening, a "safe place" for open sharing and discussion. It is not outcome-oriented. It's not even about fully understanding or comprehending what one reads or hears from the other participants. The focus is on *listening* rather than formulating a response to what another is saying. Simply hearing and accepting another's point of view and reflecting on it can inform and enlighten our own perspective in a way that debating or analyzing it cannot. The pace of conversation is slower in contemplative dialogue than in most other conversations. We are challenged to listen more carefully and approach different points of view by looking at the deeper values and issues underlying them.

Eight Principles for Entering into Contemplative Dialogue

1. Keep in mind that Bridges focuses on our "lived experience" and how the session theme connects to everyday life. Keep your comments rooted in your own experience and refrain from remarks that are overly abstract, philosophical, or theoretical.

2. Express your own thoughts knowing that others will listen and reflect upon what you say. It is helpful to use "I" statements like "I believe . . ." or "I am confused by that response." Try framing your remarks with phrases such as "My assumption is that . . ." or "My experience has been . . ." While others in the group may very well not respond to your thoughts verbally, trust that they are hearing you.

3. Pay attention to the assumptions, attitudes, and experiences underlying your initial or surface thoughts on the topic. Ask yourself questions like: "Why am I drawn to this particular part of the reading?" "What makes me feel this way?"

4. Remember to listen first and refrain from thinking about how you might respond to another's comments. Simply listen to and accept his or her thoughts on the subject without trying to challenge, critique, or even respond aloud to them.

5. Trust the group. Observe how the participants' ideas, reflections, common concerns, assumptions, and attitudes come together and form a collective group mind.

6. Reflect before speaking and be concise. Make one point or relate one experience, then stop and allow others to do the same.

7. Expect periods of silence during the dialogue. Learn to be comfortable with the silence and resist the urge to speak just because there is silence.

8. Avoid cross-talking. In time you will adjust to saying something and not receiving a response and to listening without asking a question, challenging, or responding directly. Simply speaking to the theme or idea from your own experience or perspective takes some practice. Be patient with yourself and the other members of your group and watch for deepening levels of dialogue.

These principles for contemplative dialogue are extracted from the work of the Centre for Contemplative Dialogue. For more complete information visit www.contemplativedialogue.org.

ADDITIONAL RESOURCES

A leader's guide and introductory DVD for the Bridges series are available from Ave Maria Press.

Online resources available at www.avemariapress.com include:

- Leader's Guide
- Sample pages
- Suggested Retreat Schedule
- Program Evaluation Form
- Links to other books about Thomas Merton
- Interview with Robert Toth of the Merton Institute for Contemplative Living

FROM THE MERTON INSTITUTE FOR CONTEMPLATIVE LIVING: WWW.MERTONINSTITUTE.ORG

Merton: A Film Biography (1 hour) provides an excellent overview on Merton's life and spiritual journey.

Soul Searching: The Journey of Thomas Merton is a sixty-seven-minute DVD that goes to the heart of Merton's spiritual journey through the perspective of Merton's friends, Merton scholars, and authorities on the spiritual life.

Contemplation and Action is a periodic newsletter from the Merton Institute with information about new Merton publications, programs, and events. It is free and can be obtained by visiting the institute's website or calling 1-800-886-7275.

The Thomas Merton Spiritual Development Program is a basic introduction to Merton's life and his insights on contemplative spirituality, social justice, and interreligious dialogue. Especially designed for youth, it includes a participant's workbook/journal.

Weekly Merton Reflections: Receive a brief reflection from Merton's works via e-mail each week by registering at www.mertoninstitute.org or by contacting:

The Merton Institute for Contemplative Living
2117 Payne Street
Louisville, KY 40206
1-800-886-7275

session one

THE ECOLOGY OF PARADISE

OPENING REFLECTION

PSALM 148:1–5A

> Alleluia!
>
> Praise the Lord from the heavens,
> praise him in the heights.
> Praise him, all his angels,
> praise him, all his host.
>
> Praise him, sun and moon,
> praise him, shining stars.
> Praise him, highest heavens
> and the waters above the heavens.
> Let them praise the name of the Lord.

INTRODUCTION TO THE TEXTS

Contemplative living calms our souls' inner weather as we attend to what truly matters and "forget our vain cares and enter into our own hearts."

Contemplatives co-create with others a climate for relationships of mutual peace and justice. They unite themselves with those who are creating new ecologies of kindness and interdependence among all beings.

Merton revered nature as a mirror and sacrament of an inner paradise of the heart. Nature was a channel of "heavenliness" that aroused his potential for wholeness in the midst of his life's complexities. Nature mirrored for Merton the paradise of integrity within himself to be regained by acts of love and service to all beings. He sensed that the sacred place he had always been searching for was as close as his own inner heart if he tilled it with "freedom, spontaneity, and love" and received the "new seeds of contemplation" that "every moment and every event" of his life were planting in his soul (*New Seeds of Contemplation*, p. 14).

Merton's Voice
From *No Man Is an Island*

All nature is meant to make us think of paradise. Woods, fields, valleys, hills, the rivers and the sea, the clouds traveling across the sky, light and darkness, sun and stars, remind us that the world was first created as a paradise for the first Adam, and that in spite of his sin and ours, it will once again become a paradise when we are all risen from death in the second Adam. Heaven is even now mirrored in created things. All God's creatures invite us to forget our vain cares and enter into our own hearts, which God Himself has made to be His paradise and our own. If we have God dwelling within us, making our souls His paradise, then the world around us can also become for us what it was meant to be for Adam—his paradise. But if we seek paradise outside ourselves, we cannot have paradise in our hearts. If we have no peace within ourselves, we have no peace with what is all around us. Only the man who is free from attachment finds that creatures have become his friends. As long as he is attached to them, they speak to him only of his own desires. Or they remind him of his sins. When he is selfish, they serve his selfishness. When he is pure, they speak to him of God. (pp. 115–116)

Another Voice
Teilhard de Chardin, *The Divine Milieu*

We must try everything for Christ; we must hope everything for Christ. *Nihil intentatum* (nothing not tried). That, on the contrary, is the true Christian attitude. To divinize does not mean to destroy, but to sur-create. We shall never know all that the Incarnation still expects of the world's potentialities. We shall never put enough hope in the growing unity of mankind.

Jerusalem, lift up your head. Look at the immense crowds of those who build and those who seek. All over the world, people are toiling—in laboratories, in studios, in deserts, in factories, in the vast social crucible. The ferment that is taking place by their instrumentality in art and science and thought is happening for your sake. Open, then, your arms and your heart, like Christ your Lord, and welcome the waters, the flood and the sap of humanity. Accept it, this sap—for, without its baptism, you will wither, without desire, like a flower out of water; and tend it, since, without your sun, it will disperse itself wildly in sterile roots. (pp. 154–155)

Reflect and Dialogue

What images, words, or sentences in the readings most resonate with your life's experiences? In what ways do they connect with your life?

Who or what in your life makes you feel as if you are living in paradise now?

What role does the "chorus of living things" have in your life?

To paraphrase a line by American poet Mary Oliver, what do you plan to do with the rest of your one wild and precious life?

Closing

Conclude with one of the meditations on pages 54–56 or with a period of quiet reflection.

session two
ENTERING PARADISE: THE PILGRIMAGE TO HUMAN KINDNESS

OPENING REFLECTION

PSALM 96:1–3

> O sing a new song to the Lord,
> sing to the Lord all the earth.
> O sing to the Lord, bless his name.
>
> Proclaim his help day by day,
> tell among the nations his glory
> and his wonders among all the peoples.

INTRODUCTION TO THE TEXTS

Whether we travel to Jerusalem, Mecca, or Salt Lake City, whether we return to the church where we were married or visit the house where our mothers were born, pilgrimage to places of sacred beginnings is an important component of our lives. We journey to places that represent a "golden time." For contemplatives, however, the real pilgrimage is not a "return" but a "going forward" to the Eden within our hearts where the "meaning, order, truth, and salvation" implanted in us by God can flourish to full harvest.

Merton considered one of the holiest pilgrimages he could make was his inner journey toward "the stranger as our other self." Merton's inner journey toward deeper relationships was catholic and communal

19

since he knew there was no spiritual El Dorado that he could discover alone. As human beings we are bound together in a matrix of relationships that become in themselves our "paradise isle." On the corner of two ordinary streets in the middle of a shopping district we, like Merton, can become conscious that the "gate of paradise is everywhere."

Merton's Voice
From Mystics and Zen Masters

The Bible has always taken man in the concrete, never in the abstract. The world has been given by God not to a theoretical man but to the actual beings that we are. If we instinctively seek a paradisiacal and special place on earth, it is because we know in our inmost hearts that the earth was given in order that we might find meaning, order, truth, and salvation in it. The world is not only a vale of tears. There is joy in it somewhere. Joy is to be sought, for the glory of God.

But the joy is not for mere tourists. Our pilgrimage is more than the synthetic happy-making of a vacation cruise. Our journey is from the limitations and routines of "the given"—the *Dasein* which confronts us as we are born into it without choice—to the creative freedom of that love which is personal choice and commitment. Paradise symbolizes this freedom and creativity, but in reality this must be worked out in the human and personal encounter with the stranger seen as our other self. . . .

Our task now is to learn that if we can voyage to the ends of the earth and find ourselves in the aborigine who most differs from ourselves, we will have made a fruitful pilgrimage. That is why pilgrimage is necessary is some shape or other. Mere sitting at home and meditating on the divine presence is not enough for our time. We have to come to the end of a long journey and see that the stranger we meet there is no other than ourselves—which is the same as saying that we find Christ in him.

For if the Lord is risen, as He said, He is actually or potentially alive in every man. Our pilgrimage to the Holy Sepulcher is our pilgrimage to the stranger who is Christ our fellow-pilgrim and our brother. There is no lost island merely for the individual. We are all pieces of the paradise isle, and we can find our [Saint] Brendan's island only when we all realize ourselves together as the paradise that is Christ and His Bride, God, man, and Church. (pp. 111–112)

ANOTHER VOICE
SIMONE WEIL, *THE SIMONE WEIL READER*

The children of God should not have any other country here below but the universe itself, with the totality of all the reasoning creatures it ever has contained, contains, or ever will contain. That is the native city to which we owe our love.

Less vast things than the universe, among them the Church, impose obligations that can be extremely far-reaching. They do not, however, include the obligation to love. At least that is what I believe. I am moreover convinced that no obligation relating to the intelligence is to be found among them either.

Our love should stretch as widely across all space, and should be equally distributed in every portion of it, as is the very light of the sun. Christ has bidden us to attain to the perfection of our heavenly Father by imitating his indiscriminate bestowal of light. Our intelligence too should have the same complete impartiality.

Every existing thing is equally upheld in its existence by God's creative love. The friends of God should love him to the point of merging their love into his with regard to all things here below.

When a soul has attained a love filling the whole universe indiscriminately, this love becomes the bird with golden wings that pierces an opening in the egg of the world. After that, such a soul loves the universe, not from within but from without; from the dwelling place of the Wisdom of God, our first-born brother. Such a love does not love beings and things in God, but from the abode of God. Being close to God it views all being and things from there, and its gaze is merged to the gaze of God.

We have to be catholic, that is to say, not bound by so much as a thread to any created thing, unless it be to creation in its totality. . . .

We are living in times that have no precedent, and in our present situation universality, which could formerly be implicit, has to be fully explicit. It has to permeate our language and the whole of our way of life. (pp. 112–114)

Reflect and Dialogue

What images, words, or sentences in the readings most resonate with your life's experiences? In what ways do they connect with your life?

From what class or type of person have your experiences estranged you?

To what sacred places in your biography do you consistently return, if only in your mind?

How would it change your life if you fully appreciated Simone Weil's assertion that "every existing thing is equally upheld in its existence by God's creative love"?

Closing

Conclude with one of the meditations on pages 54–56 or with a period of quiet reflection.

session three
THE HEART'S EDEN:
DISCOVERING JESUS

OPENING REFLECTION

PSALM 86:11–13

> Show me, Lord, your way
> so that I may walk in your truth.
> Guide my heart to fear your name.
>
> I will praise you, Lord my God, with all my
> heart and glorify your name for ever;
> for your love to me has been great:
> you have saved me from the depths of the
> grave.

INTRODUCTION TO THE TEXTS

William Blake's mystical sensibilities opened his mind's eye to "see the universe in a grain of sand." Merton's mystical vision of the inter-communion of all things in God transfigured his daily life by his continuing apprehension of the "energies" that flowed through his life from his continuing rediscovery of Jesus. When he was attentive, Merton experienced the "gaze of Christ upon his heart," a gaze that transfigured an ordinary task and made it holy.

One particularly illuminating and transfiguring experience in Merton's life was his ordination to the Roman Catholic priesthood as a monk of Gethsemani.

What Merton received at this momentous event was an intuition that he would remember for the rest of his life.

> God never does things by halves. He does not sanctify us patch upon patch. He does not make us priests or saints by superimposing an extraordinary existence upon our ordinary lives. He takes our whole life and our whole being and elevates it to a supernatural level, transforms it completely from within, and leaves it exteriorly what it is: ordinary.
>
> —*The Sign of Jonas*, p. 182

MERTON'S VOICE
FROM *ENTERING THE SILENCE*

Today, in a moment of trial, I rediscovered Jesus, or perhaps discovered Him for the first time. But then, in a monastery you are always discovering Jesus for the first time. Anyway, I came closer than ever to fully realizing how true it is that our relations with Jesus are something utterly beyond the level of imagination and emotion.

His eyes, which are the eyes of Truth, are fixed upon my heart. Where His glance falls, there is peace: for the light of His Face, which is the Truth, produces Truth wherever it shines. His eyes are always on us in choir and everywhere and in all times. No grace comes to us from heaven except He looks upon our hearts.

The grace of this gaze of Christ upon my heart transfigured this day like a miracle. It seems to me that I have discovered with this freedom a recollection that is no impediment to moderate action. I have felt the Spirit of God upon me and after dinner, walking along the road beyond the orchard by myself under a cobalt blue sky (in which the moon was already visible), I thought that, if only I turned my head a little, I would see a tremendous host of angels in silver armor advancing behind me through the sky, coming at last to sweep the whole world clean. I did not have to mortify this fantasy as it did not arouse my emotions but carried me along on a vivid ocean of peace. And the whole world and the whole sky were filled with a wonderful music, as it has often been for me in these days. Sitting alone in the attic of the garden house and looking at the stream shining under the bare willows and at the distant hills, I think I have never been so near to Adam's, my father's, Eden. Our Eden is the Heart of Christ. (pp. 403–404)

ANOTHER VOICE
A.M. ALLCHIN, "THE WORSHIP OF THE WHOLE CREATION"

In *Conjectures of a Guilty Bystander* Merton wrote, "If I can unite in myself the thought and devotion of Eastern and Western Christendom, the Greek and the Latin Fathers, the Russian with the Spanish Mystics, I can prepare in myself the reunion of divided Christians . . . If we want to bring together what is divided we cannot do so by imposing one division upon another or absorbing one division into another. We must contain all the divided worlds in ourselves and transcend them in Christ" [p. 20]. This is precisely what Merton has done, containing the divisions within himself and transcending them in the unity which is Christ. This is a unity that is cosmo-theandric. I dislike technical terms but this one has its uses. It brings together God, human-kind and the world into a single focus. It speaks of the worship of the whole of creation, the huge chorus of living beings.

This cosmic dimension of Merton's thought cannot be separated from the two other dimensions, human and divine, which meet in Christ in whom God, humanity and all things created are reconciled. Merton's whole effort of mastering the tradition of Christian East and West, or rather of letting himself be mastered by it, was anything but antiquarian. It was motivated by an urgent desire to enter more deeply into the life and death and rising of Christ for the sake of the world today. In his introduction to the Lectures on Ascetical and Mystical Theology [p. 9] he writes, "The mystical tradition of the Church: a collective memory and experience of Christ living and present within her. This tradition forms and affects the whole of man: intellect, memory, will, emotions, body, skills (arts), all must be under the sway of the Holy Spirit. Important human dimensions given by tradition—its incarnate character—note especially the memory." And he goes on to say that, if we do not have a healthy and conscious grasp of tradition, we shall be prey to "unhealthy and unconscious traditions—a kind of collective disposition to neurosis," a highly perceptive comment on some movements that call themselves traditionalist.

I have spoken of the mystical tradition of the Church. But I must go on at once to make the point from which Merton begins his whole teaching on the subject. There is nothing esoteric or exclusive about this tradition. It is simply the handing on of the Gospel of Christ, the faith by which the people of God have lived for 2000 years, in its deepest and most authentic form. (pp. 104–105)

Reflect and Dialogue

What images, words, or sentences in the readings most resonate with your life's experiences? In what ways do they connect with your life?

At what moments in your life have you rediscovered that "God gazes upon you"?

How would you explain to a person younger than you that there is much to be learned in "moments of trial"?

How urgent is your desire to live contemplatively for the sake of the world?

Closing

Conclude with one of the meditations on pages 54–56 or with a period of quiet reflection.

session four
DISCOVERING PARADISE WITHIN COMMUNITIES OF FORGIVENESS

OPENING REFLECTION

PSALM 103:8–12

> The Lord is compassion and love,
> slow to anger and rich in mercy.
> His wrath will come to an end;
> he will not be angry for ever.
> He does not treat us according to our sins
> nor repay us according to our faults.
>
> For as the heavens are high above the earth
> so strong is his love for those who fear him.
> As far as the east is from the west
> so far does he remove our sins.

INTRODUCTION TO THE TEXTS

Our readiness to forgive offenses and to realize our own need for pardon as we pardon another is a clear sign that God's love has triumphed in our contemplative lives. "If we are open, we will not only offer pardon to one another, but will not disdain to seek it and recognize our own desperate need of it."

Our relationships achieve holiness when we are ready to identify our lives on every level with the lives of all other human beings. Forgiveness and recognition of our need to be forgiven confirm that Love is transforming us into persons tasked with the protection of everyone's right to joy in their being alive. Olivier Clément regards our uniting ourselves to others as our life's sacred work: "The sanctified person is someone no longer separated."

MERTON'S VOICE
FROM SEASONS OF CELEBRATION

We are a community of pardon, not a community of judgment. We are told not to judge one another, and we must not. We must not judge in such a way as to reject and condemn. . . .

We have a duty to pardon, because it is through us that God wishes to pardon all sinners.

In building a community of pardon, which is the temple of God, we have to recognize that no one of us is complete, self-sufficient, perfectly holy in himself. No one can rest in his own individual virtues and interior life. No man lives for himself alone. To live for one's self alone is to die. We grow and flourish in our own lives in so far as we live for others and through others. What we ourselves lack, God has given them. They must complete us where we are deficient. Hence we must always remain open to one another so that we can always share with each other.

Often the good that is given us by God is given us only to be shared with another. If He sees that we will not pardon and will not be open, that we will not share, then the good is not given us. But to him in whom there is the greatest readiness to share with all most is given. The greatest of gifts then is this openness, this love, this readiness to accept and to pardon and to share with others, in the Spirit of Christ. If we are open we will not only offer pardon, but will not disdain to seek it and recognize our own desperate need of it.

Openness is the sign of the Spirit's presence, for openness is the sign of love. How characteristic was the action of Pope John XXIII who, when asked after his election what he intended to do as Pope, simply walked over to a window and flung it open. (pp. 229–230)

ANOTHER VOICE
OLIVIER CLÉMENT, *THE ROOTS OF CHRISTIAN MYSTICISM*

The sanctified person is someone no longer separated. And he is only sanctified to the extent that he understands in practice that he is no longer separated from anyone or anything. He bears humanity in himself, all human beings in their passion and their resurrection. He is identified, in Christ, with the 'whole Adam.' His own 'self' no longer interests him. He includes in his prayer and in his love all humanity, without judging or condemning anyone, except himself, the last of all. He is infinitely vulnerable to the horror of the world, to the tragedies of history being constantly renewed. But he is crushed with Christ and rises again with him, with everyone. He knows that resurrection has the last word. Deeper than horror is the Joy.

> Those who have been judged worthy to become children of God and to be born from on high of the Holy Spirit . . . not infrequently weep and distress themselves for the whole human race; they pray for the 'whole Adam' with tears, inflamed as they are with spiritual love

for all humanity. At times also their spirit is kindled with such joy and such love that, if it were possible, they would take every human being into their heart without distinguishing between good and bad. Sometimes too in humility of spirit they so humble themselves before every human being that they consider themselves to be the last and least important of all. After which the Spirit makes them live afresh in ineffable joy.

—Psuedo-Macarius,
Eighteenth Homily, 9: 34, 79

Our spiritual life and death are at stake in our relations with others. We are reminded of Saint John of the Cross: "On the last day we shall be judged by our love." (pp. 273–274)

Reflect and Dialogue

What images, words, or sentences in the readings most resonate with your life's experiences? In what ways do they connect with your life?

Whom in your life are you finding it impossible to forgive?

Who in your life loved you most by forgiving you?

How would you explain to a person younger than you that "our spiritual life and death are at stake in our relations with others"?

Closing

Conclude with one of the meditations on pages 54–56 or with a period of quiet reflection.

session five
FINAL INTEGRATION 1: CONTEMPLATIVE LIVING AS INNER EXPERIENCE

OPENING REFLECTION

PSALM 40:6

> How many, O Lord my God,
> are the wonders and designs
> that you have worked for us;
> you have no equal.
> Should I proclaim and speak of them,
> they are more than I can tell!

INTRODUCTION TO THE TEXTS

In the last years of his life Merton studied the powerful insights into Sufism in the work of the Iranian psycho-analyst A. Reza Arasteh in his book *Final Integration in the Adult Personality* (1965). Arasteh's thesis confirmed an intuitive conviction of Merton's that had guided his mature spirituality: Loyalty to the truth of God's creative fecundity demands continuing transcendence of any vision of God that is limited to the aspirations of one particular historical period or group.

Merton's mature contemplative living pushed him toward a breakthrough in his consciousness and behavior that transcended his western education, his American national identity, and his needs for security and self-affirmation on western cultural terms. Merton's continuing existential question was "How can I mature enough to realize communion with all beings?"

Living contemplatively as mature adults will find us acquiring practical means to answer the call to widening relationships. These relationships will always be instigated and grounded in our personal relationship to God whom we eventually discover is a "subject" and a "who." Contemplatives surrender to life's energies that force a transcending of their egos so that optimally their awareness and responses to life are one with God's awareness. God wholly penetrates their personalities, even the unconscious dimension of their being: "I sleep but my heart watches and loves."

MERTON'S VOICE
FROM CONTEMPLATION IN A WORLD OF ACTION

Final integration is a state of transcultural maturity far beyond mere social adjustment, which always implies partiality and compromise. The man who is "fully born" has an entirely "inner experience of life." He apprehends his life fully and wholly from an inner ground that is at once more universal than the empirical ego and yet entirely his own. He has attained a deeper, fuller identity than that of his limited ego-self, which is only a fragment of his being. He is in a certain sense identified with everybody: or in the familiar language of the New Testament . . . he is "all things to all men." He is able to experience their joys and sufferings as his own, without however becoming dominated by them. He has attained to a deep inner freedom—the Freedom of the Spirit we read of in the New Testament. He is guided not just by the will and reason, but by: "spontaneous behavior subject to dynamic insight." [Merton is here quoting from Arasteh's *Final Integration in the Adult Personality*.]

Again, the state of insight which is final integration implies an openness, an "emptiness," a "poverty" similar to those described in such detail not only by the Rhenish mystics, St. John of the Cross, and the early Franciscans, but also by the Sufis, the earliest Taoist masters, and Zen Buddhists. Final integration implies the void, poverty, and non-action which leave one entirely docile to the "Spirit" and hence a potential instrument of unusual creativity. (p. 225)

ANOTHER VOICE
IRA PROGOFF, *AT A JOURNAL WORKSHOP*

We each go down individually into the well of our life. The well of each personal existence is separate and distinct from the other. Each of us must therefore go down our own well, and not the well of someone else's life. We find, however, that when, as individuals, we have gone very far down into the well of our own life, we come to an underground stream that is the source of all the wells. Since the wells of our personal existence are each separate from every other, there are no separations here. There are no walls or dividers in the underground stream. We are all connected here in the unitary continuum of being.

We each must go through our own personal existence, but when we have gone deeply enough we find that we have gone through our personal life beyond our personal life. This is the transpersonal connection, which we experience in the underground stream. We each work toward it individually within the context of our own life history. When we reach it, however, we do not remain in the depths. Those waters have the effect of renewing our energies and give us access to abundant resources of our life. We draw upon these sources and carry them back with us to the surface of the well where we incorporate them in living the next time-unit of our lives.

The symbol of the well and the underground stream thus carries us through a continuing cycle of experiences. While the outer events of our lives take place at the surface of the well, we go inward to the underground stream to reach our deep sources, and to have the revitalizing experience of reconnecting ourselves with the larger unity of life. Having broken through the walls of individuality to enter the deep source, we then return to live our personal existence in the world of external reality. (pp. 33–34)

Reflect and Dialogue

What images, words, or sentences in the readings most resonate with your life's experiences? In what ways do they connect with your life?

How has contemplative dialogue affirmed for you Merton's intuition in *The Asian Journal* that "our real journey is interior"?

How would you explain in your own words Saint Bernard of Clairvaux's intuition that, in the life of the Spirit, "We must dig our own wells"?

What disparate areas of your daily living most need integration?

Closing

Conclude with one of the meditations on pages 54–56 or with a period of quiet reflection.

session six

FINAL INTEGRATION 2: THE LOSS OF SELF IN FULL RIPENESS

OPENING REFLECTION

PSALM 23:3B–4

> He guides me along the right path;
> he is true to his name.
> If I should walk in the valley of darkness
> no evil would I fear.
> You are there with your crook and your staff;
> with these you give me comfort.

INTRODUCTION TO THE TEXTS

The universal mystery of dying and being reborn to a new life, of the grain of wheat needing to die to bring forth fruit, brings perennial insight into the process of personal transformation toward the fullness of union with the Creator. Contemplative living requires that we die to what is less integral to human experience and live attentive to the desires of our deepest hearts. The "less" integral and important is not always evil but must be surrendered or integrated into who we are becoming as we make conscious choices for a more holistic spiritual life. As we move through deeper relationships, we order our lives to the "one thing necessary" for Love to be all in all. What is best in our daily living never needs to be surrendered: everyone and everything we love moves

forward to maturity with us, securely fastened in the
pockets of our hearts.

MERTON'S VOICE
FROM *CONTEMPLATION IN A WORLD OF ACTION*

Dr. Arasteh describes the breakthrough into final integration in the language of Sufism. The consecrated
term in Sufism is *Fana*, annihilation or disintegration, a
loss of self, a real spiritual death. But mere annihilation
and death are not enough: they must be followed by
reintegration and new life on a totally different level.
This reintegration is what the Sufis call *Baqa*. The process of disintegration and reintegration is one that in-
volves a terrible interior solitude and an "existential
moratorium," and crisis and an anguish that cannot be
analyzed or intellectualized. It also requires a solitary
fortitude far beyond the ordinary, "an act of courage
related to the root of all existence." It would be utterly
futile to try to "cure" this anguish by bringing the "patient" as quickly and as completely as possible into the
warm bosom of togetherness. Carl Jung, with whom
Arasteh has much in common, says this:

> The development of the person is at once a
> charism and a curse because its first fruit is the
> conscious and unavoidable segregation of the
> individual from the undifferentiated and un-
> conscious herd. This means isolation, and there
> is no more comforting word for it. Neither fam-
> ily nor society nor position can save him from
> the fate, nor yet the most successful adaptation
> to his environment.

Seen from the viewpoint of monastic tradition, the pattern of disintegration, existential moratorium and reintegration on a higher, universal level is precisely what monastic life is meant to provide. In the strictly limited, authoritarian caste societies of medieval Europe, of India, of China, of Japan, the individual lived within extreme restriction in a framework that denied him social mobility. But the unusual person, from any caste, could become a monk. If he were able to live as an authentic beggar and pilgrim, accept the sacrifices, the insecurities, the risks, the challenges of the solitary adventure, he was freed from social limitations. He was on his own, on the road, in the jungle or in the desert, and he was entitled to develop in his own way, indeed to devote himself with passionate dedication to a freedom even from the limits of his contingency as a creature: he could get lost in the light of eternity, provided he found the way! (pp. 227–228)

ANOTHER VOICE

A. REZA ARASTEH, *FINAL INTEGRATION IN THE ADULT PERSONALITY*

In Near Eastern culture the mechanism of rebirth in final integration takes place in two major psychological steps, both of which are interrelated. In brief, the Sufis assert that a seeker faces two major tasks: to dissolve his present status (*fana*), then reintegrate again. "Unless you are first disintegrated, how can I reintegrate you again?" (Rumi). Disintegration here refers to the passing away of the conventional self, reintegration means rebirth in the cosmic self. *Fana* is the removal of the "I"; *baqa* the process of becoming "I." Instead

41

of being related to the partial self-intellect, reintegration means bringing to light the secrets of the total personality. In a practical sense it means cleansing one's consciousness of what Rumi calls fictions, idols and untruths and purifying the heart of greed, envy, jealousy, grief and anger so that it regains its original quality of becoming mirror-like to reflect the reality within it. *Fana* means, in fact, a liberation from self-intellect, and *baqa* is an affirmation of truth and love. In going through the process of rebirth the principle of individual differences is recognized. In other words, rebirth requires: (a) detachment from such external values as fame, and wealth, (b) the selection of a guide, (c) detachment from inner veils, (d) intentional isolation, (e) traveling and arriving at the state of nothingness, and (f) integration into "everythingness." (pp. 368–369)

Yet in conclusion, one can say that regardless of language, cultural and temporal differences, all styles of life have adopted the same goal of experiencing final integration, and moreover, the reality behind the ways they have adopted is similar in all. The name makes no difference; it is the experience which is the same. The common denominator, the process of break-through, comes with the inner experience of life. This is essential for its result, not its process. It results in "certainty," in positivity and a mature attitude. It is also synthesized in a state of receptivity known as "no-knowledge" in Taoism, "emptiness" in Zen Buddhism, "nothingness" and "poverty" in Sufism, and "the void" in the writings of Al-Ghazzali. (p. 374)

Reflect and Dialogue

What images, words, or sentences in the readings most resonate with your life's experiences? In what ways do they connect with your life?

To what have you had to die in the past in order to become who you are today?

From what "fictions, idols and untruths" has your life through grace, prayer, and experience been cleansed?

Recall moments in your life when you experienced a process of "disintegration followed by reintegration."

Closing

Conclude with one of the meditations on pages 54–56 or with a period of quiet reflection.

session seven
FINAL INTEGRATION 3: CONTEMPLATIVE LIVING AND PEACEMAKING

OPENING REFLECTION

PSALM 103:19–22

> The Lord has set his sway in heaven
> and his kingdom is ruling over all.
> Give thanks to the Lord, all his angels,
> mighty in power, fulfilling his word,
> who heed the voice of his word.
>
> Give thanks to the Lord, all his hosts,
> his servants who do his will.
> Give thanks to the Lord, all his works,
> in every place where he rules.
> My soul, give thanks to the Lord!

INTRODUCTION TO THE TEXTS

The behavioral goal of final integration in the contemplative life is becoming a peacemaker. Thomas Aquinas wrote that we cannot give what we do not already have, so unless the lion and the lamb have reclined together in our own being, we cannot bring peace to others. Becoming a peacemaker is the inner work of every day, a labor of making even incremental choices that transcend the world of violence in which we find ourselves. Our personal heart-work for peace is never finished. We must always be stretching forward toward the prize of uniting ourselves with God's will, which is that we become instruments of God's peace.

MERTON'S VOICE
FROM *CONTEMPLATION IN A WORLD OF ACTION*

The man who has attained final integration is no longer limited by the culture in which he has grown up. He has embraced all of life . . . He has experienced qualities of every type of life: ordinary human existence, intellectual life, artistic creation, human love, religious life. He passes beyond all these limiting forms, while retaining all that is best and most universal in them, "finally giving birth to a fully comprehensive self." [Merton is quoting Arasteh.] He accepts not only his own community, his own society, his own friends, his own culture, but all mankind. He does not remain bound to one limited set of values in such a way that he opposes them aggressively or defensively to others. He is fully "catholic" [universal] in the best sense of the word. He has a unified vision and experience of the one truth shining out in all its various manifestations, some clearer than others, some more definite and more certain than others. He does not set these partial views in opposition to each other, but unifies them in a dialectic or an insight of complementarity. With this view of life he is able to bring perspective, liberty, and spontaneity into the lives of others. The final integrated man is a peacemaker, and that is why there is such a desperate need for our leaders to become such persons of insight. . . . (pp. 225–226)

Another Voice
A. Reza Arasteh, *Final Integration in the Adult Personality*

In recent Western thought the problem of final integration is becoming more recognized in our age of increasing anxiety. It has been noted under such names as "spontaneous expression without reservation" (Fromm), "peak experience" (Maslow), "becoming one's self" (Rogers), "intensive visionary experience" (A. Huxley), "dynamic insight" (Fromm-Reichman) and "autonomous individuality" (Reisman).

In short, the state of final integration is the end of vertical growth of the adult personality and the beginning of horizontal expansion into creativity. It exceeds the objectivization of the ego and is concerned with the liberation of the ego. This state is further marked by intense awareness of various spheres of reality: the existential reality of essence versus the natural reality of appearance; the reality of meaning versus the reality of oneness. In a similar way there exist sub-spheres of reality within the cultural reality that appear in physical, spiritual and social patterns. It is significant that all Western and Eastern ways of attaining maturity in the adult personality have recognized as an essential quality the ability to become aware of multiple realities. (pp. 361–362)

Reflect and Dialogue

What images, words, or sentences in the readings most resonate with your life's experiences? In what ways do they connect with your life?

In what ways have you heard the call to become a peacemaker?

In your own words explain to yourself why peacemaking is akin to "seeing God."

Who in your life can you acknowledge as a peacemaker?

Closing

Conclude with one of the meditations on pages 54–56 or with a period of quiet reflection.

session eight
A TRANSFORMING VISION OF LOVE'S TRUE HORIZONS

OPENING REFLECTION

PSALM 33:20–22

> Our soul is waiting for the Lord.
> The Lord is our help and our shield.
> In him do our hearts find joy.
> We trust in his holy name.
>
> May your love be upon us, O Lord,
> as we place all our hope in you.

INTRODUCTION TO THE TEXTS

Contemplative living is a response to a call to wholeness and integration that is implanted at birth in the nature of the human being. We are called to become holy in the depths of who we most truly are. The Orthodox theologian Olivier Clément has been a major voice in this series arising from his magnificent book *The Roots of Christian Mysticism.* The debt to him must now be repaid by allowing his voice to introduce the final texts of Bridges to Contemplative Living with Thomas Merton.

> By the intervention of the mystery of Christ and of the witness of his followers, a state of death is transformed into a state of resurrection. In Christ the world becomes Eucharist.

In him we can transfigure the world by integrating it into the human consciousness of the Risen Christ who offers resurrection to everyone and everything.

Sanctity imparts the divine light not only to our bodies but to the whole cosmic environment. Today, when history itself is raising the ultimate questions, we are called to what Simone Weil termed a "holiness of genius" that is able to communicate the light to the very foundations of culture.

—*The Roots of Christian Mysticism*, p. 228

MERTON'S VOICE
FROM *SEASONS OF CELEBRATION*

The monastic life cannot be defined by any one of its parts. It cannot be reduced to one of its aspects, any more than the life of any living organism can be fully explained by one of the vital functions that that organism performs. Man is a rational animal, they say. But he does not exist merely in order to grow, or eat, or work, or think, or even to love. On the contrary, growth, nutrition, work, thought and love all unite in promoting and increasing the existential depth of the mysterious reality which is the individual person, a concrete, free, inexplicable being endowed with powers whose depth no mind but God's can ever fathom. The human person, then, is a free being created with capacities that can only be fulfilled by the vision of an unknown God. And the monk is a person who has been unable to resist the need to seek this unknown God in the hiddenness and silence of His own inscrutable wisdom.

All the substance of the monastic vocation, therefore, is buried in the silence where God and the soul meet, not as object and subject, but as "one Spirit." The very essence of monasticism is hidden in the existential darkness of life itself. And life is inexplicable, irreducible to systematic terms. It is only understood by being lived. The best we can say is that the monk is one who goes out to the frontiers of liberty and of existence, seeking the impossible, seeking the vision which no man can see without dying. And yet this idea must immediately be corrected, for it is at once exaggerated and misleading. For when the monk is able to reach a certain degree of wisdom, he realizes that he had already found God by becoming mysteriously unwise. And then the circle is closed, and the monastic life begins. (pp. 23-24)

ANOTHER VOICE
MATTHEW KELTY, O.C.S.O., *SERMONS IN A MONASTERY*

In the morning, then, I rise with Christ and with Christ I go to pray and with Christ I chant the office and with Christ I break my fast with bread and coffee. With Christ I commune in secret prayer in my heart, with Christ I read the Good Book, go to work. With Christ I love my brother and bear the heat and suffer pain and know heartache, endure loneliness, and keep silent, suffer rebuke and quench anger. With Christ I walk the earth and count the stars at night. The same sun as shone on him shines on me. The moon that has lighted his Gethsemane lights mine. The same rain that fell on his holy head falls on mine, runs down my neck—I walk the earth he walked, live the life he lived.

If these things happen to me in Christ, and I do these things in Christ, then I do them with the whole human family. For with every person who ever lived I lie down each night and sleep. I rise in the morning. I work. I pray. I read. I suffer. With all of humanity, past, present and to come. In Christ. That being so, I share in some way with the total life of the whole earth, of the whole universe. I touch eternity and eternal life in God by the trivial things I do every day, in every breath I draw, every time I have a drink of water. . . .

I sat on the hill and watched a Brother slowly going up and down the bottom with the tractor, seeding corn. It was as beautiful a morning as God ever made. Above me in the trees seven birds were singing in wild abandon, for sheer joy. Beside me in the fenced-in meadow two brown horses were racing back and forth up to their knees in wet grass, kicking and frolicking. The clouds above were massive white and gold with purple eye shadow. A light breeze was blowing in from the east, moving the light mist ever so gently, for the cool hollows were shrouded in fog. Who was playing most or best? The horses in the dewy field, the birds in the sycamores, the clouds in the sky? The Brother who had gone forth to sow his seed? Or God in his heaven? It does not matter, for all were playing, each in his own way, and a great joy was shared by heaven and earth. I went to sing Prime. I thought the pitch high and the choir flat and I was mad. But that did not matter either. I was singing with the angels. That was real, singing with Christ in his glory, singing with everyone on the earth, with the Brother on the tractor, with the Brother dying in the infirmary, with every person on earth: the good and the bad, the virtuous and the dissolute, the sober and the drunken, the free and the imprisoned, the rich and the poor, people dying and leaving the world, people being born and just coming into it. I sing with them all in Christ.

If this is not perfect joy there is none. What matter if my own heart be barren and empty, my mind a sterile waste, my own life full of fuss and fury. It does not matter. You do not have to be holy to love God. You only have to be human. Nor do you have to be holy to see God in all things. You have only to play as a child with an unselfish heart, and so be lost in rapture at the great reality that lies hidden just under the surface of things. (pp. 44–47)

Reflect and Dialogue

What images, words, or sentences in the readings most resonate with your life's experiences? In what ways do they connect with your life?

Express your understanding of "contemplative living."

What impact has contemplative dialogue had on your relationships?

In what ways has your spiritual life changed since you have crossed these "bridges" with Thomas Merton and your dialogue partners?

Closing

Conclude with one of the meditations on pages 54–56 or with a period of quiet reflection.

CONCLUDING MEDITATIONS

A.

O Sweet Irrational Worship

Wind and a bobwhite
And the afternoon sun.

By ceasing to question the sun
I have become light,

Bird and wind.

My leaves sing.

I am earth, earth

All these lighted things
Grow from my heart.

A tall, spare pine
Stands like the initial of my first
Name when I had one.

When I had a spirit,
When I was on fire
When this valley was
Made out of fresh air
You spoke my name
In naming Your silence:
O sweet, irrational worship!

I am earth, earth

My heart's love
Bursts with hay and flowers.
I am a lake of blue air
In which my own appointed place

Field and valley
Stand reflected.

I am earth, earth

Out of my grass heart
Rises the bobwhite.

Out of my nameless weeds
His foolish worship.

Thomas Merton
The Collected Poems, pp. 344–345

B.

Real spring weather—these are the precise days when everything changes. All the trees are fast beginning to be in leaf, and the first green freshness of a new summer is all over the hills. Irreplaceable purity of these few days chosen by God as His sign! Mixture of heavenliness and anguish. Seeing "heavenliness" suddenly, for instance, in the pure white of the mature dogwood blossoms against the dark evergreens in the cloudy garden. "Heavenliness" too of the song of the unknown bird that is perhaps here only for these days, passing through, a lovely, deep, simple song. Pure—no pathos, no statement, no desire, pure heavenly sound. Seized by this "heavenliness" as if I were a child—a child's mind I have never done anything to deserve to have and that is my own part in the heavenly spring. Not of this world, nor of my making. Born partly of physical anguish (which is really not there, though. It goes quickly). The sense that "heavenliness" is the real nature of things, not their nature, not "in themselves," but the fact that they are a gift of love, and freedom.

Thomas Merton
Dancing in the Water of Life, p. 99

C.

Ode 34

The simple heart finds no hard way, good thought finds no wounds.
Deep in the illuminated mind is no storm.
Surrounded on every side by the beauty of the open country, one is free of doubt.

Below is like above.

Everything is above.
Below is nothing, but the ignorant think they see.

Now you know grace. It is for your salvation.
Believe and live and be saved.

"The Odes of Solomon"
The Other Bible, p. 282

SOURCES

The Readings from the Psalms are from *The Psalms: An Inclusive Language Version Based on the Grail Translation from the Hebrew.* Published through exclusive license agreement by G.I.A. Publications, Inc. Copyright © 1963, 1986 by The Grail (England).

FROM THOMAS MERTON

The Collected Poems of Thomas Merton. New York: New Directions, 1977.

Contemplation in A World of Action. New York: Doubleday, 1971.

Dancing in the Water of Life. Journals, Vol. 5. Robert E. Daggy, ed. San Francisco: HarperSanFrancisco, 1997.

Entering the Silence. Journals, Vol. 2. Jonathan Montaldo, ed. San Francisco: HarperSanFrancisco, 1996.

Faith and Violence: Christian Teaching and Christian Practice. Notre Dame, IN: University of Notre Dame Press, 1968.

"Merton's Sufi Lectures to Cistercian Novices, 1966-68." Bernadette Dieker, transcriber.

Merton & Sufism: The Untold Story. Baker, Rob and Henry, V. Gray, eds. Louisville, KY: Fons Vitae Press, 1999.

Mystics and Zen Masters. New York: Farrar, Straus, Giroux, 1967.

New Seeds of Contemplation. New York: New Directions Publishing Corp., 1962.

No Man Is An Island. New York: Harcourt Brace Jovanovich Publishers, 1955.

Seasons of Celebration. New York: Farrar, Straus and Giroux, 1965.

The Sign of Jonas. New York: Harcourt Brace Jovanovich, Publishers, 1953.

ANOTHER VOICE

Allchin, A. M. "The Worship of the Whole Creation: Merton and the Eastern Fathers." *Merton & Heyschasm: The Prayer of the Heart.* Bernadette Dieker and Jonathan Montaldo, eds. Louisville, KY: Fons Vitae, 2003.

Arasteh, Abdol Reza. *Final Integration in the Adult Personality.* Leiden, Netherlands: E. J. Brill, 1965.

Barnstone, Willis, ed. *The Other Bible.* New York: Harper Collins Publishers, 1984.

Clément, Olivier. *The Roots of Christian Mysticism.* New York, New City Press, 1993.

Kelty, O.C.S.O., Matthew. *Sermons in a Monastery.* William O. Paulsell, ed. Kalamazoo, MI: Cistercian Publication, Inc., 1983.

Chardin, Teilhard de. *The Divine Milieu.* New York: Harper and Row Publishers, 1965.

Progoff, Ira. *At A Journal Workshop.* New York: G.P. Putnam's Sons, 1975. For information on the Intensive Journal program as well as Ira Progoff's books and audio materials, please contact Dialogue House Associates, 800-221-5844, www.intensivejournal.org.

Weil, Simone. *The Simone Weil Reader.* George A. Panichas, ed. Mt. Kisko, NY: Moyer Bell Limited, 1977.

another voice
Biographical Sketches

A. M. Allchin, a friend and correspondent of Thomas Merton, is an honorary professor in the Department of Religious Studies at the University of Wales, Bangor. He was formerly canon of Canterbury Cathedral and librarian of Pusey House, Oxford. He has published extensively in the field of Celtic spirituality and theology, and lectures in his field all over the world. Throughout his career, Allchin has been involved with ecumenism and the relationship between Eastern Orthodoxy and the Christianity of the West.

Abdol Reza Arasteh (1927–1992) was born in Shiraz, Iran. He had studied both Eastern and Western psychology and seemed to bridge Merton's earlier interest in psychology with his later interest in Sufism, Zen, and other Eastern traditions. He lived a number of years in the United States and became a citizen in 1976.

Willis Barnstone is a prolific poet, memoirist, and editor. His literary translation of the New Testament, *The New Covenant: The Four Gospels and Apocalypse*, was published in 2002. A Guggenheim Fellow and Pulitzer Prize finalist in poetry, he is Distinguished Professor at Indiana University.

Olivier Clément (1921–2009) was a French Orthodox theologian who lectured at St. Sergius Institute in Paris. In addition to his magisterial *The Roots of Christian Mysticism*, he has authored *Three Prayers: The Lord's Prayer, O Heavenly King, Prayer of Saint Ephrem; On*

Human Being: Spiritual Anthropology; and *You Are Peter: An Orthodox Reflection on the Exercise of Papal Primacy.*

Teilhard de Chardin, S.J. (1881–1955), was a visionary French Jesuit, paleontologist, biologist, and philosopher, who spent the bulk of his life trying to integrate religious experience with natural science, most specifically Christian theology with theories of evolution. Included among his best-known works are *The Phenomenon of Man* and *Building the New Earth.*

Matthew Kelty, O.C.S.O., is a Cistercian monk at the Abbey of Gethsemani, Kentucky. He was a missionary priest in New Guinea before entering the abbey as a novice under Thomas Merton. After some years at Gethsemani he returned to New Guinea as a hermit where he wrote his first book *Flute Solo.* After returning to the monastery, he became chaplain to guests and retreatants. His spiritual conferences after the last office of Compline are deservedly famous.

Ira Progoff (1921–1998) was an American psychotherapist, best known for his development of the Intensive Journal Method. His main interest was in depth psychology and particularly the humanistic adaptation of Jungian ideas to the lives of ordinary people. He founded Dialogue House in New York City to help promote this method.

Simone Weil (1909–1943) was a mystic and philosopher, French and Jewish. Andre Gidé called her "the most spiritual writer of this century." Her works in English include *Gravity and Grace, The Need for Roots, Waiting for God,* and *Openness and Liberty.*

The Merton Institute for Contemplative Living is an independent, non-profit organization whose mission and purpose is to awaken interest in contemplative living through the works of Thomas Merton and others, thereby promoting Merton's vision for a just, peaceful, and sustainable world.

Robert G. Toth served as the executive director of the Merton Institute for Contemplative Living from 1998 to 2009. He currently serves the institute as director of special initiatives.

Jonathan Montaldo has served as the associate director of the Merton Institute for Contemplative Living, director of the Thomas Merton Center, and president of the International Thomas Merton Society. He has edited or co-edited nine volumes of Merton's writing including *The Intimate Merton, Dialogues with Silence,* and *A Year with Thomas Merton.* He presents retreats internationally based on Merton's witness to contemplative living.